PR

OUR PRIESTS

A GUIDE TO PRAYING FOR THE PRIESTHOOD
IN UNION WITH
MARY, QUEEN OF THE CLERGY

THIRD EDITION

INCLUDES MEDITATIONS ON THE PRIESTHOOD
FOR THE MYSTERIES OF THE ROSARY.

A MEDITATED ROSARY FOR VOCATIONS TO THE
PRIESTHOOD AND CONSECRATED LIFE.

THE STATIONS OF THE CROSS FOR PRIESTS.

BY MONSIGNOR PETER DUNNE
AND VICKI HEROUT

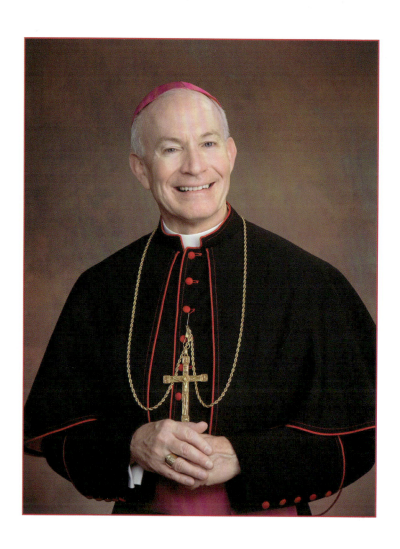

ONE CHURCH
ENCOUNTERING JESUS
EQUIPPING DISCIPLES
LIVING MERCY

June 2024

Dear Friends in Christ,

I am happy to recommend this third edition of "Praying for Our Priests." I am very grateful to the members of Maria Regina Cleri for the publication of this helpful resource.

Over the years, tens of thousands have prayed with these books, supporting the lives of our priests. It is impossible to calculate the strength and encouragement offered to priests and those discerning a call to the priesthood by the prayers of so many. Thank you for the support you will give as you use these prayers and meditations.

With best wishes, I am

Sincerely yours in Christ,

Most Reverend George J. Lucas
Archbishop of Omaha

| **Imprimatur for Praying for Our Priests:** | Most Reverend Elden F. Curtiss
Archbishop of Omaha
October 1, 2008
Omaha, Nebraska | |

| **Nihil Obstat for Praying for Our Priests:** | Fr. Joseph Taphorn
Censor Librorum
Archdiocese of Omaha |

| **Imprimatur for Praying for Vocations:** | Most Reverend George J. Lucas
Archbishop of Omaha
October 9, 2012
Omaha, Nebraska | |

| **Nihil Obstat for Praying for Vocations:** | Reverend Matthew Gutowski
Censor Librorum
Archdiocese of Omaha |

This third edition of **Praying for Our Priests** combines the above two books into one volume. All content in each section remains the same as in the original books.

ISBN: 979-8-218-45328-2

Dedication:

To all the faithful priests and consecrated souls who have spent their lives in the service of the Gospel of Jesus Christ.

Cover Image:

The image of Our Lady of Victory was chosen for the cover of this booklet because it so beautifully manifests Mary's loving tenderness and solicitude for her Son, Jesus, Who is the Eternal High Priest. Her tenderness and solicitude for Him extends itself to include every priest son for all time and eternity.

Photography:

Robert Ervin — Ervin Photography; Front & back cover • Vocations image, page 45 • Monstrance, page 74 Crucifix, page 77 • The Stations of the Cross, beginning on page 81

Alida Choat — Alida's Picture Pages; The Resurrection, page 96.

Mary Vesting St. John — by Br. Claude Lane, OSB, Mount Angel Abbey, page 13. Available from www.altarandhome.org.

Book Design — Patrick J. Ervin

IN TRIBUTE

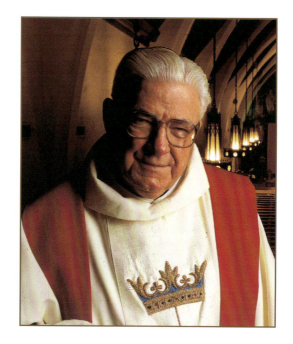

Monsignor Peter Dunne
Founding Chaplain, Maria Regina Cleri
1919-2015

"May your devotion to Mary grow from day to day so that when you mount the hill of sacrifice, you will know the joy of having Mary, the Mother of the Priest, at your side."

From an exhortation to a brother priest by Monsignor Dunne,
September 23, 1944 - his Ordination Day

PRAYER TO "DIVINE LOVE" FOR PRIESTLY CHARITY

O Divine Love, we come before You to pray and intercede for our priests that they may become the living presence of Your love among us.

O Divine Love, enter and take complete possession of their hearts that all their affections may be toward charity.

O Divine Love, enter and be ever first in their minds that all their thoughts may be charitable.

O Divine Love, enlighten their intellects that they may always discern that which is most charitable.

O Divine Love, imbue all their words that they may always speak that which is most charitable and encouraging.

O Divine Love, inhabit their wills that they may always will and do that which is most charitable.

O Divine Love, animate all their senses and movements that they may only hear and see with Your senses and always respond with Your charity.

O Divine Love, penetrate to the very core of their souls, consume all their darkness, until You, O Divine Love, are able to radiate pure love through them to all they meet.

O Mary, Mother of Divine Love, pray for our priests.

TABLE OF CONTENTS

Prayer for Divine Charity for Priests	VIII
Introduction	3
Prayers of the Holy Rosary	5
The Holy Hour for Priests or Vocations	7

Praying for our Priests

Optional Prayers for Priests for Various Needs	9
The Joyful Mysteries for Priests	15
The Luminous Mysteries for Priests	21
The Sorrowful Mysteries for Priests	27
The Glorious Mysteries for Priests	33
General Intercessions for Priests	39
Concluding Prayers	42

Praying for Vocations

	43
The Joyful Mysteries for Vocations	47
The Luminous Mysteries for Vocations	53
The Sorrowful Mysteries for Vocations	59
The Glorious Mysteries for Vocations	65
General Intercessions for Vocations	71
Concluding Prayers	72

Benediction Hymns and Prayers	73

The Stations of the Cross	78
Appendix	97
Works Cited	98
References/Footnotes	99
Ordering Information	102

INTRODUCTION

There can be no more fruitful investment in the life of Holy Mother Church than time spent in prayer for Her priests and vocations to the priesthood.

This project had its origin in the early days of 2006 when Monsignor Peter Dunne, recovering from a long and critical illness, experienced a deepening awareness of the need to pray for his brother priests in Purgatory. At the same time, Vicki Herout, his longtime caregiver, spiritual daughter, and coworker in many projects, began to realize in her own prayers an intense and persistent call to pray for the priesthood. Eventually, they brought together a group that has continued to meet regularly to pray for priests. This booklet, initially compiled as an aid to this prayer group, has been adapted for use by individuals as well as small and large groups in a variety of settings.

The meditations on the priesthood that you will read in this booklet came out of the hearts and prayers of the authors — out of the heart of Monsignor Dunne who loved and lived his priesthood to the fullest for over seventy years — and out of the many months his coauthor spent praying, meditating, and writing before the Blessed Sacrament. These prayers are meant for all to pray — priests, consecrated, and laity — but they are written with the special purpose of providing insights into the life of a priest and into the mystery of the priesthood itself that will awaken and encourage in the laity a desire to pray for priests and for holy vocations.

As we prepare to go to print with this third edition of our book, we continue to be amazed at the growing multitude of prayer warriors that the Lord is raising up around the world to pray for His beloved priests. And we are more aware than ever of the need our priests have to be confirmed, supported and appreciated in their vocation.

There are some significant layout changes in this third edition, as we have chosen to combine our Praying for Our Priests and our Praying for Vocations books into one volume. The meditations and prayers in each section, though, are the same as in previous editions of both books. We hope you will find the new layout easy to maneuver.

While we, the apostolate of Maria Regina Cleri, miss our beloved founding Chaplain, Monsignor Peter Dunne, since his passing in 2015, we continue to look to him for guidance and are confident of his prayers for this work. Monsignor Dunne prayed untiringly for his brother priests in this life, and we can be sure he continues this ministry in eternity. May we all commit ourselves to pray for the priesthood with the same devoted love, care, and concern that he had. And may our Lord bless you for your faithful prayers.

THE PRAYERS OF THE HOLY ROSARY

The Apostles' Creed

All: I believe in God, the Father Almighty, Creator
of Heaven and earth; and in Jesus Christ,
His only Son, our Lord, Who was conceived
by the Holy Spirit, born of the Virgin Mary,
suffered under Pontius Pilate, was crucified, died,
and was buried.

He descended into hell. On the third day
He arose again from the dead; He ascended into
Heaven, and is seated at the right hand of God,
the Father Almighty; from thence He shall come
to judge the living and the dead.

I believe in the Holy Spirit, the Holy Catholic Church,
the Communion of Saints, the forgiveness of sins,
the resurrection of the body, and life everlasting.

Amen.

Our Father, three Hail Marys, Glory Be

The Mysteries of the Rosary

Hail Holy Queen

All: Hail Holy Queen, Mother of Mercy, our life, our
sweetness and our hope. To thee do we cry, poor
banished children of Eve. To thee do we send up our
sighs, mourning and weeping in this valley of tears.
Turn then, most gracious Advocate, thine eyes of
mercy toward us, and after this, our exile,
show unto us the Blessed Fruit of thy womb, Jesus.
O clement, O loving, O sweet Virgin Mary!

Leader: Pray for us O Holy Mother of God,

All: That we may be made worthy of the promises of Christ.

Leader: Let us pray.

All: O God, Whose only begotten Son, by His life, death,
and resurrection, has purchased for us the rewards
of eternal life, grant we beseech Thee, that meditating
on these mysteries of the Most Holy Rosary of
the Blessed Virgin Mary, we may imitate what they
contain and obtain what they promise, through
the same Christ our Lord.
                                    Amen.

THE HOLY HOUR FOR PRIESTS OR VOCATIONS

If these prayers are being said with Exposition of the Blessed Sacrament, the following Exposition hymn and prayers before the Blessed Sacrament may be done. If not, begin with the Prayer to the Holy Spirit on the next page.

EXPOSITION OF THE BLESSED SACRAMENT (Kneel)

"O Salutaris Hostia"

O Salutaris Hostia

Quae coeli pandis ostium:

Bella premunt hostilia,

Da robur, fer auxilium.

Uni trinoque Domino,

Sit sempiterna gloria,

Qui vitam sine termino

Nobis donet in patria.

Amen.

"O Saving Victim"

O saving Victim, opening wide

The gate of heav'n to man below.

Our foes press on from ev'ry side;

Thine aid supply; Thy strength bestow.

To Thy great name be endless praise,

Immortal Godhead, One in Three,

Oh, grant us endless length of days,

In our true native land with Thee.

Amen.

Recite the following prayers:

O Sacrament Most Holy, O Sacrament Divine,
All praise and all thanksgiving be every moment Thine!
(3 times)

PRAYER TO THE HOLY SPIRIT

Leader: Come, Holy Spirit, fill the hearts of Your faithful.

All: **Kindle in them the fire of Your love.**

Leader: Send forth Your Spirit, and they shall be created,

All: **And You shall renew the face of the earth.**

Leader: Let us pray:

All: **O God, Who by the light of the Holy Spirit, did instruct the hearts of the faithful, grant that by that same Holy Spirit, we may be truly wise and ever rejoice in His consolation through Christ our Lord.**

Amen.

PRAYERS FOR THE HOLY FATHER

Prayers for the Holy Father, Pope (N.), for his health, his safety and his intentions — **Our Father, Hail Mary, Glory Be**

SERRA PRAYER FOR VOCATIONS

O God, Who wills not the death of a sinner, but rather that he be converted and live, grant we beseech You, through the intercession of the Blessed Mary, ever Virgin, Saint Joseph, her spouse, Saint Junipero Serra, and all the saints, an increase of laborers for Your Church, fellow laborers with Christ to spend and consume themselves for souls, through the same Jesus Christ, Your Son, Who lives and reigns with You, in the unity of the Holy Spirit, God forever and ever.

Amen.

The Holy Hour for Priests continues on Page 9.
The Holy Hour for Vocations continues on Page 43.

OPTIONAL PRAYERS FOR PRIESTS FOR VARIOUS NEEDS

PRAYER FOR THE PRIESTHOOD

All: O Most Holy Trinity,
Father, Son, and Holy Spirit,
we adore You and we love You with all our hearts.
We come before You,
humbly and prayerfully,
to intercede for all Your holy priesthood.
(We lift up in a special way all the priests who reside in our diocese.)

Father, we give You thanks with grateful hearts for the faithful witness of so many priest-sons. Bless and protect them, Father, hold them and shelter them in the palm of Your Hand.

Jesus, Eternal High Priest,
we lift up to You those priests who suffer and struggle,
those who are heavy-burdened,
and those who have lost their way.
Bless and heal them, Jesus,
You Who have said,
"Come to Me all you who find life burdensome…
 and I will give you rest."

Holy Spirit, Eternal Love of the Father and the Son,
pour out Your Love, Your Gifts, and Your Graces on every priest of God. Strengthen them, Holy Spirit, fill them and assure them of our love.

O Mary, Mother of Jesus,
Queen and Mother of all priests,
intercede for these special sons of yours.
Hold them in your Immaculate Heart, cradle them in your arms,
protect them from every evil bent against them,
teach them to love, and lead them at last
into the arms of your Son in Heaven.

Amen.

Pope Francis has said, "All of the love God has in Himself, all the beauty that God has in Himself, all the truth that God has in Himself, He gives to the family."[1] With this beautiful reflection, the Holy Father reminds us of how absolutely essential the family unit is to the Church and how critically important is the priest's role in guiding the families he serves to healthy relationship within the Church. In this light, we offer the following prayer:

PRAYER FOR PRIESTS AND FAMILES

All: Eternal Father, You have graciously willed to design the family of man after the loving relationships within the Most Holy Trinity. You have set before us the example of the Holy Family of Nazareth, and have given us holy priests that they might lead and guide the faithful in the way of loving, familial relationship in Your Church.

Father, we pray for all priests as they labor to serve our families in an unbelieving and hurting world. May they serve with listening and compassionate hearts, gently guiding families, especially those most troubled, to all truth and to the fullness of communion with the family of the Church.

We pray, too, that all families will strive to live the truth in their homes, that they will pray for their priests, support and appreciate them, look to them for guidance in this world, and through them, come to know the family of the Church as a true part and a true extension of their own family.

We pray all of this in Your Name, Father, from whom every family in Heaven and on earth takes its name.[2]

Immaculate Heart of Mary, Queen of all Priests, Queen of all Families, pray for us.

Amen.

1 *Pope Francis, World Meeting of Families, 2015*   2 *See Ephesians 3:15*

PRAYER FOR THE URGENT NEEDS OF PRIESTS (Option 1)

All: Lord Jesus, You are the Eternal High Priest Who, from age to age, has called men to follow in Your footsteps, to sacrifice at Your holy altar, and minister to Your people through Your gift of the priesthood. It is through Your priests that we can see Your face, Jesus, and we are so grateful!

But, we come before You now, Lord, lifting up to You those priests who, through false accusations or their own weakness and sin, can no longer remain in active ministry. Lord, You know they are many. Give us hearts to love, respect, and pray for these priests and to provide assistance to those whom You have called to care for them, troubled and struggling in their many mental, physical, spiritual, and emotional needs. We beg You, Lord, through the intercession of the Immaculate Heart of Mary, mother of all priests, give us hearts for these suffering ones whom You yet love and hold dear in Your own Sacred Heart. We ask this in Your Holy Name, Jesus.

Amen.

PRAYER FOR THE URGENT NEEDS OF PRIESTS (Option 2)

All: O Lord Jesus Christ, Eternal High Priest and exemplar of priestly holiness and dignity, we are grateful to You for having chosen certain men for the ministerial priesthood by which You continue to instruct, admonish, forgive, nourish and strengthen Your Church.

We are sorely aware of the great need of priests in our time to be confirmed in their sacred calling so that they may continue confidently in their ministry of mediating Your graces to men and of representing them before Your august majesty.

Relying on the intercession of Holy Mary, mother of priests, and of Saint Joseph, her beloved spouse, we beg Your help for the priests who are the most troubled, tempted, discouraged and suffering.

May the noble and sacred office of the priesthood, which has too often been reviled and scorned, regain its admirable stature in the sight of all men for Your greater honor and glory, and for the sanctification and salvation of Your people.[3]

Amen.

Leader: Eucharistic Heart of Jesus, Model of the Priestly Heart,
All: Have mercy on all priests.

READING FROM SCRIPTURE (Stand)

The Gospel of the day or the Gospel for the coming Sunday may be used or the leader may choose from the Scripture readings suggested in the Appendix.

PAUSE FOR SILENT REFLECTION (Sit)

(A short homily/meditation may be given)

THE HOLY ROSARY FOR PRIESTS

Mary Vesting St. John

MARY VESTING ST. JOHN

In this icon, Mary places
a white priest's stole on St. John.
Mary is both a symbol of the Church, who bestows
the Priesthood of Jesus upon men chosen to
continue His ministry, *and* the Mother of the Priest
(Mater Cleri). Thus, Holy Mother Church clothes
her priests in holiness, and the Blessed Mother
intercedes for their vocations.

Br. Claude Lane, OSB

The Joyful Mysteries for Priests

The Annunciation

The angel announces to Mary that she will conceive in her womb and bear a Son Who will be called Son of the Most High. Mary's "Yes", her great *fiat*, reverberates for all time and eternity; and, the Word is made flesh — God becomes Man and dwells among us.

We pray that all young men who are being called by God to the priesthood will give their consent to the Will of God.

We pray that all priests will truly love and cherish their participation in the Sacred Priesthood, conscious that their *fiat*, like Mary's, resounds through all time and eternity: "You are a priest forever according to the order of Melchizedek." [4]

The Visitation

Mary, with the Infant Jesus in her womb, travels in haste to the home of Elizabeth. The infant John the Baptist in the womb of Elizabeth leaps for joy, and Elizabeth herself is filled with the Holy Spirit at the sound of Mary's voice and the presence of the Lord so near.

We pray that all priests might live and love to bring Jesus to others — that they might be the merciful, healing presence of Christ as they visit the sick, the elderly, the imprisoned, and the dying.

We pray that all priests might work reverently and tirelessly to protect and defend all human life.

The Birth of Jesus

Mary gives birth to the Prince of Peace, the Light of the World, in the darkness and poverty of a stable in Bethlehem. Through her, the Eternal Word of the Father comes as a little child to bring us the Father's message of love and forgiveness. This is the true gift of Christmas.

We pray that all priests will place their hope and trust in this message of the Father's love and forgiveness that they, too, may become as little children of God.

And we pray that, as they live out this Christmas message in their own lives throughout the year, they will inspire in others the hope Christ came to bring us.

The Presentation

Mary and Joseph present Jesus in the Temple according to the Law of Moses. Simeon, a holy and devout man "awaiting the consolation of Israel" [5], takes the Child in his arms and blesses God, telling Mary that her Son will be a "sign that will be contradicted" [6] and that her own heart will be pierced.

We pray that all priests — "signs of contradiction" in the world today — might be messengers of God's love and peace and consolation to the whole world.

We pray that all priests might unite themselves to the Heart of Mary when their hearts, too, are pierced by the pain and suffering that is both around and within them.

5 *Luke 2:25 (NAB)*   6 *Luke 2:34 (NAB)*

The Finding of the Child Jesus in the Temple

Mary and Joseph, after three days of anxious searching, find the Child Jesus sitting among the teachers in the Temple. He returns with Mary and Joseph to Nazareth and is obedient to them.

We pray that all priests may be found teaching the faith in word and action wherever they may be.

We pray that all priests might turn to Mary and Joseph with obedient and childlike trust in all their needs as Jesus surely did, and that, like Jesus, they may grow in wisdom and age and grace in the sight of God.[7]

7 Luke 2:52 (NAB)

The
Luminous Mysteries
for Priests

The Baptism of Jesus

The Son of God, in profound humility, approaches John the Baptist and descends into the waters of the Jordan to be baptized by him. The Beloved Son sanctifies for all time the waters of baptism "while the Spirit descends on Him to invest Him with the mission which He is to carry out." [8]

We pray that all priests, like Jesus, will humbly and lovingly accept the mission of their vocation to serve and suffer for the people of God.

We pray that every priest might be a voice in the spiritual wilderness of today's society, calling souls to repentance and inviting them to meet and recognize Jesus as John the Baptist did — "Behold, the Lamb of God, who takes away the sin of the world." [9]

8 *Rosarium Virginis Mariae, 21*   9 *John 1:29 (NAB)*

The Wedding Feast at Cana

Mary, with simplicity and genuine concern, says to her Son, "They have no wine." [10] And with faith in her Divine Son, she turns to the servants at the wedding and says, "… do whatever He tells you." [11] Jesus responds with the first of His public miracles — changing water into wine.

We pray that all priests, with loving simplicity, will follow Mary's counsel to "… do whatever He tells you." They, too, will see miracles.

We pray for all priests as they teach and prepare couples for the Sacrament of Marriage.

We pray that every priest will cherish his own spousal relationship with Holy Mother Church and live it out with sensitivity, chastity, and love.

10 John 2:3 (NAB)   11 John 2:5 (NAB)

The Proclamation of the Kingdom of God

Jesus came to reconcile mankind to the Father, ushering in this ministry of reconciliation with the first words of His public ministry, "… the Kingdom of God is at hand. Repent and believe in the Gospel."[12]

We pray that all priests will be gentle and compassionate ministers of the Sacrament of Reconciliation.

We pray that all priests throughout their lives of ministry will pray and study the Gospels with fervor, and that as they break open the Gospel message for the faithful each day, they will preach it with truth and boldness and live it with love.

The Transfiguration

Jesus takes Peter, James, and John up the mountain where, in the presence of Moses and Elijah, He reveals to them His glory, thus strengthening their faith for the road to Calvary which lies ahead.

We pray that all priests can and will immerse themselves in prayer daily and experience in this the love and peace of God that strengthens them for their daily trials.

We pray that as each priest prays and listens to the voice of the Beloved Son, he will be transfigured into a more perfect image of the Love of Christ, his eyes ever on Jesus and the glory that follows a life lived in fidelity to Him.

The Institution of the Holy Eucharist

Jesus institutes the Eucharist and the ministerial priesthood at the Last Supper. These two — the Eucharist and the priesthood — can NEVER be separated.

The priest must find his happiness — his joy — in his oneness with Christ. This oneness realizes its fullest expression at the moment of Consecration at every Mass when the priest, *in persona Christi*, offers himself as both priest and victim for the salvation of souls.

We pray that every priest will believe in the True Presence of Jesus in the Holy Eucharist and will faithfully and reverently celebrate Mass each day, adoring the Lord Whom he holds in his hands and witnessing his love for Christ in the Most Blessed Sacrament.

We pray for priests preparing souls of all ages for their First Communion and for those priests preparing seminarians for the Sacrament of Holy Orders.

The Sorrowful Mysteries
for Priests

The Agony in the Garden

Jesus, in fervent prayer in the Garden of Gethsemane, sweats blood as He sees the suffering, torture, and humiliation that awaits Him. He feels the weight of the sins of mankind and knows that His sacrifice will be a scandal to some, misunderstood and rejected by others. In the midst of this dark and bitter agony, Jesus surrenders — "Not My will, [Father,] but Thine, be done." [13]

It is the privilege and obligation of every priest everywhere to give his life for the sanctification and salvation of souls. We pray that all priests will surrender themselves into the hands of the Father each day, no matter what it costs.

We pray that every priest can place his trust fully in the Lord, especially in the midst of darkness, misunderstanding, or humiliation — when his best efforts for the good of souls appear to be in vain.

13 Luke 22:42 (RSV)

The Scourging at the Pillar

Jesus is bound to a pillar and His Sacred Flesh is mercilessly scourged. His Precious Blood flows freely from His open wounds.

We pray that all priests will remain faithful to the discipline of celibacy and be diligent by their words and their example in promoting purity and chastity in all vocations.

We pray that every priest who, through weakness and neglect of his relationship with Christ, has fallen into sin, ignored or rejected the teachings of the Church, or abandoned his vocation, may repent and return to the merciful love of God.

The Crowning with Thorns

Jesus' Sacred Head is pierced deeply with a crown of thorns. Again, His Precious Blood flows freely for us. He is mocked and spat upon, but the "man of sorrows, despised and rejected, opens not his mouth." [14]

We pray that all priests will strive for and cherish the virtue of humility, shunning every show of pride and seeking always to carry out their duties with humble and sincere obedience, in the sure knowledge that the least assignment for the Kingdom is no less than the greatest when all is done for the love of God.

We pray that all priests, like Jesus, will look with kindly and fatherly eyes on the great and the small, the rich and the poor alike in their ministry.

14 *Isaiah 53:3,7 (RSV)*

The Carrying of the Cross

Jesus carries His heavy Cross up the hill of Calvary, falling again and again under the weight of our sins. He is exhausted, in terrible pain, and surrounded by brutality.

We pray here especially for priests who, being falsely accused or having actually fallen in some way, must yet endure scorn, gossip, and rejection rather than the love and prayer they need.

We pray that every priest, when he sees a fallen brother, will come to his aid with the fraternal charity and prayer he needs for support and healing.

The Crucifixion and Death of Jesus

Jesus came into the world to show us the way to the Father. Now, in His final hour, hanging in agony on the Cross, He reveals the depth of God's love and mercy by giving His life to redeem us from sin and death.

We pray for all priests as they administer the Anointing of the Sick and carry *Viaticum* to the dying.

For all priests who are now on their deathbed and those who will die this day, we ask for the grace of final perseverance. We pray, too, that through their union with Christ on the Cross, they may find the strength to forgive all who have offended them throughout their ministry.

And we pray for the souls of all priests in Purgatory.

The
Glorious Mysteries
for Priests

The Resurrection

Jesus Christ is Risen! We sing Alleluia!!

Here is the foundational truth of our faith. Jesus has broken the power of death, reconciled God and mankind, and opened for all the gates of Heaven.

We pray that all priests who suffer through painful trials will unite themselves to the suffering Christ that they may come to know with Him the light and joy of the Resurrection.

We pray that all priests will celebrate the Resurrection with Easter joy every Sunday.

The Ascension

If the truth of the Resurrection is the foundation of our faith, the Ascension is surely the basis for our hope.

Jesus came to show a lost and fallen humanity the way to the Father. Now, as He returns to the Father, He takes our restored humanity with Him, leaving His apostles with the instructions to carry the Gospel into the whole world, making disciples of all the nations and baptizing in the name of the Father and of the Son and of the Holy Spirit.[15] To this very day, every priest is ordained and sent for this same purpose.

We pray for all priests as they open the doors of salvation to countless souls through the saving waters of Baptism.

We pray for the safety and protection of all priests, especially missionary priests who carry the Gospel message into dangerous and sometimes violent areas of the world.

We lift up, in a special way, those priests who will shed their blood for the Gospel of Jesus Christ.

The Descent of the Holy Spirit

The Holy Spirit descends in tongues of fire on the apostles, filling them with the Love of God, sanctifying them, and empowering them to go forth to announce and explain the Word of God with authority.[16] In a similar way, the Holy Spirit descends on every priest at his ordination to remain with him for all time in his ministry to the people of God.

We pray for all priests as they prepare souls for a new infilling of the Holy Spirit at Confirmation.

We pray that every priest might prayerfully beg for the gifts of the Holy Spirit and seek opportunities to gather with his brother priests and the faithful to pray, to praise God, and to call forth the gifts of the Holy Spirit to help build up the Body of Christ.

The Assumption

Mary is assumed body and soul into Heaven.

The language of true love — the proof of true love —
is sacrifice. Like her crucified Son Who sacrificed all
to redeem us, Mary has sacrificed her entire life to
God. And when, at the foot of the Cross, Jesus said to
her, "Woman, behold, your son," [17] she took into her
heart not just John, but all of humanity and, in
a special way, every priest for all time and eternity.

We pray that every priest will cherish deeply his filial
relationship with Mary, that he will love her, turn to
her in all his needs, spread devotion to her, and at last
commend himself into her maternal arms at the hour
of his death.

17 John 19:26 (NAB)

The Coronation

Mary, most humble of all God's children, is crowned Queen. She is exalted forever over every creature in the heavens above and on earth below!

As Queen and Mother of all priests, Mary remains at the side of each of her sons throughout his life of ministry, guiding, inspiring, and exhorting him, and interceding for him before the Throne of God.

We pray for the holiness and fidelity of every priest from the day of his ordination to the day he, too, enters eternity where he may take his place with Mary and the entire Communion of Saints to experience forever the incomprehensible Love of God. *"Deus meus et omnia …* my God and my all!"

GENERAL INTERCESSIONS FOR PRIESTS

(All of the following intercessions may be used or the leader may select from the list)

Leader: For the Holy Father, Pope (N.), protect him, Lord, and fill him with love and courage. Let him be a sign to the whole world that he is truly the Vicar of Christ, the successor of Peter, we pray to the Lord …

All: **Lord hear our prayer.**

Leader: For all shepherds of the Church, that they may have hearts after the Heart of the Good Shepherd, always obedient to the Holy Father and all bishops in communion with him, we pray to the Lord …

All: **Lord hear our prayer.**

Leader: For all priests, that they may be filled with the gifts of the Holy Spirit as they listen, preach, and minister to the people of God, we pray to the Lord …

All: **Lord hear our prayer.**

Leader: For all priests, that they may always teach, defend, and remain faithful to the truths of the Catholic Church, and be willing to speak up or stand their ground when these truths are challenged, we pray to the Lord …

All: **Lord hear our prayer.**

Leader: That all priests, as they celebrate Mass, might approach the altar with great love for Christ and a deep sense of reverence for the Sacred Mysteries they are about to enter into, we pray to the Lord …

All: **Lord hear our prayer.**

Leader: That all priests, wherever they may be, will always be enlightened, inspired, and compassionate ministers of the Sacraments, we pray to the Lord …

All: **Lord hear our prayer.**

Leader: That all priests responsible for teaching in our schools may be gifted to teach with clarity and conviction as they open the truths of the faith to the young, we pray to the Lord …

All: **Lord hear our prayer.**

Leader: That all priests will make every effort to pray and study the Scriptures and grow in their knowledge and understanding of the teachings of the Church so as to be effective preachers of the Gospel, we pray to the Lord …

All: **Lord hear our prayer.**

Leader: For all priests who guide and direct souls, especially those priests responsible for directing the souls of their brother priests, that they may be filled with the gifts of the Holy Spirit, especially wisdom and prudence, and be enlightened and equipped for this ministry, we pray to the Lord …

All: **Lord hear our prayer.**

Leader: For all priests who have grown old in the service of the Lord and His Church, that they may be lovingly sustained and cared for in all their needs, we pray to the Lord …

All: **Lord hear our prayer.**

Leader: For all priests, that they may always know the love, support, and encouragement of their brother priests, especially in their hour of need, we pray to the Lord …

All: **Lord hear our prayer.**

Leader: For all priests, that they may be faithful to a life of prayer and that they may experience in their prayer the love of God which surpasses all understanding, we pray to the Lord …

All: **Lord hear our prayer.**

Leader: That all priests will always advocate, protect, and defend the sanctity of all human life, we pray to the Lord …

All: **Lord hear our prayer.**

Leader: That all priests will teach, promote, and help make available to the faithful the approved devotions of the Church, we pray to the Lord …

All: **Lord hear our prayer.**

Leader: That all priests will defend and remain faithful to the discipline of celibacy, especially in a world that does not value this sacrifice, we pray to the Lord …

All: **Lord hear our prayer.**

Leader: For the fidelity and sanctity of every priest, that through his life of prayer and oneness with Christ, his example may draw the faithful in his care to a deeper relationship with Christ, we pray to the Lord …

All: **Lord hear our prayer.**

(Optional) **Pause to add own intentions for priests.**

All: **Our Father who art in Heaven hallowed be Thy name; Thy Kingdom come, Thy will be done, on earth as it is in Heaven. Give us this day our daily bread and forgive us our trespasses as we forgive those who trespass against us. And lead us not into temptation, but deliver us from evil.** **Amen.**

CONCLUDING PRAYER

Leader: Let us pray:

All: **O my Jesus, I beg You on behalf of the whole Church: Grant it love and the light of Your Spirit, and give power to the words of priests so that hardened hearts might be brought to repentance and return to You, O Lord.**

Lord, give us holy priests; You Yourself maintain them in holiness. O Divine and Great High Priest, may the power of Your Mercy accompany them everywhere and protect them from the devil's traps and snares which are continually being set for the souls of priests. May the power of Your Mercy, O Lord, shatter and bring to naught all that might tarnish the sanctity of priests, for You can do all things.[18] **Amen.**

Continue to Benediction Hymns and Prayers on page 73

PRAYING FOR VOCATIONS

*"…prayer for vocations should be
continuous and trusting."*

Pope Benedict XVI

World Day of Prayer for Vocations

May, 2009

*"A vocation is a call of invitation.
It is important that we pray for vocations
since the answer to an invitation from the Father
is always a grace.
We pray particularly to Mary
who gives us the model response to a
life-changing invitation from God."*

Archbishop George J. Lucas
Archbishop of Omaha

INTRODUCTION

In the Mysteries of the Rosary, we contemplate the life, death, and resurrection of Jesus. But, if we look carefully with the eyes of faith, we may also see the life of a vocation to serve the Lord in His Church unfolding in the rhythm of the mysteries, following the path of the life of Jesus.

In the Joyful Mysteries, we first see the seed of vocation appearing, the "infant" vocation, and we pray for its nurturing in devout homes, parishes, and schools.

In the Luminous Mysteries, the Mysteries of Light, we contemplate the vocation as it takes its first steps into the light of the Church, and we pray for prayerful discernment.

In the Sorrowful Mysteries, we call to mind Jesus' words, "…unless a grain of wheat falls to the [earth] and dies, it remains a grain of wheat, but if it dies…"[1] We pray for young men and women as they enter into formation, preparing to give their lives in service to the Church, the Mystical Body of Christ.

Finally, in the Glorious Mysteries, we contemplate in the Resurrection of Jesus the glorious entrance of the newly ordained or professed into the life of Holy Mother Church, and we pray for their mission, service, and fidelity.

Let us turn our eyes, then, to Mary and join with her in praying to the Master of the Harvest that He may send an abundance of laborers into His Holy Vineyard.

THE HOLY ROSARY FOR VOCATIONS

"Speak, Lord, your servant is listening."

"It was not you who chose me,

but I who chose you

and appointed you to go and bear fruit,

fruit that will last…"

(John 15:16)

The
Joyful Mysteries
for Vocations

The Annunciation

The angel Gabriel was sent by God to a virgin named Mary of the town of Nazareth, greeting her and announcing that she would bear a son who would be called Son of the Most High. Mary was "greatly troubled" and questioned, "How can this be…?"[2] But trusting the Lord, she responded, "Let it be done to me according to your word."[3] Thus does the Father's plan for our salvation come to pass.

And just as the Incarnation of the Son of God was in the Father's plan of salvation from all eternity, so every true vocation to serve the Lord is another part of this plan — a part of His mission to bring the Good News of our salvation to the world.

We pray that all young men and women who hear God calling to them in their hearts and are "questioning" or "greatly troubled," will, as Mary did, place their trust in the Lord and say with Mary, "Let it be done to me according to your word."

2. Luke 1:34   3. Luke 1:38

The Visitation

Mary enters the house of Zechariah and her greeting reaches the ears of Elizabeth. The infant in Elizabeth's womb leaps for joy and she exclaims, "Who am I that the mother of my Lord should come to me? Blessed are you who believed that what was spoken to you by the Lord would be fulfilled."[4]

Scripture says she is "blessed" who believed, but so often, those who become aware that God may be calling them to the priesthood or consecrated life begin to doubt, even fear. We pray for all who sense that God is calling them, that they will believe…and, in believing, be blessed…and being blessed, will be filled with the sheer joy of being chosen.

4. *Luke 1:43, 45*

The Birth of Christ

Mary gives birth to the Son of God. The Word made flesh becomes visible in a stable in Bethlehem. The Holy Family of Jesus, Mary, and Joseph make their home in Nazareth.

We pray in this mystery for all families, for it is here in the devout living of the Faith that the seed of a vocation to the priesthood or consecrated life may first be planted and nurtured.

We pray that all parents will have a deep love and respect for one another, thus establishing a loving Christian environment for their family. We pray that they will be respectful and obedient to the Church, diligent in living and teaching the Faith, and holy in their practice of devotion.

And we pray that mothers and fathers will pray for vocations — in the Church and in their own families — gently encouraging sons and daughters to pray and consider whether they, too, may be called to the priesthood or consecrated life.

The Presentation

Mary and Joseph present the infant Jesus in the Temple. They are met there by Simeon, a "holy and devout man,"[5] and Anna, who "worshipped night and day"[6] in the Temple. Called forth by the Spirit, both came to greet the infant Messiah.

We pray here for the Church, the parish environment, in which every "infant vocation" is presented.

We pray for holy and devout priests whose witness of joy and zeal in living out their priestly calling will invite young men to consider whether they, too, might be called to the priesthood.

We pray that there may be many generous souls in every parish who "worship night and day," that their prayers to the Master of the Harvest might produce an abundant harvest and nurture the vocations developing in their midst.

Finally, we pray that every parish, as a family, might be a witness to the truth that all must know, love, and serve the Lord in order to fulfill and be fulfilled in every Christian vocation.

5. *Luke 2:25*   6. *Luke 2:37*

The Finding of the Child Jesus in the Temple

When Mary and Joseph return from the Feast of Passover in Jerusalem, Jesus remains behind. After three days of searching, they find Him "in the temple, sitting among the teachers, listening to them and asking them questions."[7]

We pray for all our Catholic schools, home schools, catechetical and youth ministry programs, that in all these environments, parents, teachers and youth ministers, priests and consecrated, will take time to teach about vocations in the Church and pray with the youth for their own vocations, thus opening young minds and hearts to the many possibilities. We pray that, by their word and example, those who minister to youth will encourage them to consider a life in service to the Lord.

The Luminous Mysteries for Vocations

The Baptism in the Jordan

Jesus is baptized by John in the waters of the River Jordan. "The heavens were opened and…the Spirit of God descended like a dove upon him. And a voice came from the heavens, saying, 'This is my beloved Son, with whom I am well pleased.'"[8]

At the beginning of every lived vocation to the priesthood or consecrated life is the need to acknowledge that one may be called and to respond with prayerful discernment.

We pray for holy vocations directors, that, immersed in a life of prayer themselves, they will be able to guide those who are being called to the priesthood or consecrated life to attentive spiritual listening, discerning, and responding.

We pray also that every bishop will be kindly and attentive to the needs of each of the young men and women in his diocese who are discerning a vocation in service to the Church.

The Wedding Feast at Cana

Mary, aware that the young couple at the wedding had run out of wine, says to her Divine Son, "They have no wine."[9] And to the servants at the wedding, she says, "Do whatever He tells you."[10] Jesus responds to her faith with His first public miracle — turning water into wine.

We pray here for all parents that, as they strive to live out their own holy vocation to marriage, they will lovingly and willingly give their parental blessing to a son's or daughter's expressed desire for a vocation in service to the Lord - that they will say from their hearts with Mary, "Do whatever He tells you." They will be greatly blessed.

We pray, too, that all spiritual directors guiding young men and women who are discerning vocations may lead them to a proper understanding of the roles of spiritual fatherhood and motherhood as these roles are lived out in the priesthood and consecrated life.

9. John 2:3   10. John 2:5

The Proclamation of the Kingdom of God

When Jesus called His disciples, He simply said, "Follow me…"[11] Peter, James, John, Andrew, Matthew — in fact, all the apostles — got up, left what they were doing and followed Him. Why? Because the sound of His voice reached not just their ears, but their hearts as well.

We pray that all who are being called to a life in service to the Church may grow deeper in their life of prayer and union with God. Their acceptance and willingness to go forth, to answer this special call to discipleship, will be the fruit of their time in prayer — of hearing His voice and falling in love with the One who calls.

11. Matthew 4:19

The Transfiguration

Jesus leads Peter, James, and John up the mountain where He is transfigured before their eyes and converses with Moses and Elijah. Peter exclaims, "Lord, it is good for us to be here…"[12]

We pray here for all seminaries, convents, and houses of formation, that, immersed in and living the life envisioned by their holy founders, and ever faithful to the teachings of the Church, they may be authentically attractive to the one seeking the right place to live out his or her call to serve the Lord, that he or she may truly and rightfully say with Peter, "Lord, it is good for [me] to be here."

The Institution of the Holy Eucharist

Jesus, at the Last Supper, says, "This is my Body…
this is my Blood,"[13] leaving for us a perpetual memorial
of His suffering and death. What a magnificent gift for
us to cherish!

God is love, and love seeks union. We pray that,
through frequent reception of the Eucharist and time
spent adoring the One who is Love, those who are
being called will at last be able to surrender their lives
entirely to the Lord and follow Him. "My heart is
ready, O God, my heart is ready…"[14]

13. Matthew 26:26-28   14. Psalms 57:7

The Sorrowful Mysteries for Vocations

The Agony in the Garden

Jesus, in the Garden of Gethsemane, was in agony and, in his human nature, struggled over what lay ahead. "Father, if it is possible, let this cup pass me by…"[15] And there appeared an angel from Heaven to strengthen Him.

We pray for all men and women who, having entered formation for the priesthood or consecrated life, are now uncertain, filled with doubt or struggling with their vocation. We pray that they will remain faithful to prayer and that the Lord will send His ray of light and encouragement into their minds and hearts that they may truly know the Father's will and, like Jesus, find peace in surrendering to it.

The Scourging at the Pillar

Jesus is bound to a pillar and His sacred body is scourged and torn. Only a few hours earlier, at the Last Supper, Jesus had said to His apostles, "This is my Body, which is given up for you."[16]

Young men and women entering formation for a life in service to God must, in a certain sense, begin the process of giving themselves up for others. It is not that they are scourged or beaten or that they lose their personality or identity. Yet, in a very personal way, each must begin to die to self so that he or she may prepare to live in imitation of Christ who gave Himself up for the Church.

We pray for all young men and women in formation as they accept the gift of celibacy and begin to live its discipline. We pray that they may understand and learn to live joyfully the role of spiritual fatherhood or motherhood in the Church and come to say with Jesus, "This is my body, which is given up for you."

The Crowning with Thorns

Jesus is crowned with thorns and He is mocked and spat upon. The Son of God takes on our sins of pride with the crown of thorns and shows us the path of true humility.

We pray that those in formation may be led, through the process of prayer and spiritual direction, to a deeper knowledge of themselves that they may begin to recognize and overcome that selfishness so embedded in our fallen human nature. And we pray that, as they become more focused on the needs of others, Jesus will truly open their eyes and ears and hearts to the needs of His Mystical Body, the Church.

The Carrying of the Cross

Jesus takes up His cross, embracing it as the Father's will for Him, and sets out on the path to Calvary. Falling again and again under His burden, He rises each time, His eyes fixed on the Father in Heaven and the glory to come.

Young men and women, at this point, have come far in their journey. They have prayed and discerned their call, entered formation, and renounced themselves in order to serve the needs of others. They must now, with Jesus, take up their cross in earnest and set out on their path. They must embrace this road to Calvary as their way of life with its daily crosses and hardships, always pressing on to the joy that lies ahead. It will be a life-long process; they will fall, and they will get up again. We pray that, through their fidelity to prayer, they will always know the presence of Christ who walks with them to help shoulder the burden.

The Crucifixion and Death of Jesus

"Unless the grain of wheat falls to the earth and dies, it remains just a grain of wheat…but, if it dies, it produces much fruit."[17] Jesus, the Son of God, obedient unto death, takes on the sins of mankind and dies on the cross for us. His death is the glorious culmination of His life, lived in perfect surrender and obedience to the will of the Father.

This life of total self-surrender and obedience is also the glorious culmination of discernment and formation of the young men and women preparing to serve the Church. They now enter willingly the life-long process of dying to self in order to live in surrender to the will of the Father, to live wholly in the service of others, to live in a love so strong that it overcomes all obstacles. They are ready for ordination or final profession. Let us pray for these men and women with all our hearts as they prepare to make this sacrifice for us.

The Glorious Mysteries for Vocations

The Resurrection

Jesus Christ rises, glorious and triumphant on Easter Sunday. He has conquered death. He lives forever!

And just as Jesus bursts forth, glorious and radiant, from the tomb, so does the newly ordained or professed come forth into the dazzling light of Holy Mother Church. They, too, are radiant — eager to live out their calling, and the Church surrounds them with her love and prayers.

Let us pray in fervent thanksgiving to the Master of the Harvest who, in His great love and mercy, has provided laborers for the harvest.

The Ascension

Jesus, before He ascended into heaven, said to His apostles, "Go out to all the nations, baptizing in the name of the Father, and of the Son, and of the Holy Spirit...and know that I am with you to the end of the age."[18]

The young man or woman, newly ordained or professed, wherever he or she will serve, is truly sent out to "all the nations." From small country churches to great universities, from the seclusion of the cloister to large city parishes to the poorest missions of distant continents, they go forth to live and bear witness to the Gospel, to share the Good News of our salvation, that all may come to know and believe.

Let us pray for these young men and women that they will continue to grow ever deeper in their love for God and remain faithful to the Gospel as they take on their duties, giving themselves to the needs of the universal Church.

18. Matthew 28:19-20

The Descent of the Holy Spirit

The Spirit of God descends in tongues of fire on the apostles and they are filled with the gifts of the Holy Spirit. With the fire of holy zeal, they go forth to announce the Gospel to the nations.

The newly ordained or professed may say with great zeal in his or her heart, "Here I am, Lord, I come to do Your will." But the will of God is costly, and zeal can fade in the face of reality.

We pray for a new and continuous outpouring of the gifts of the Holy Spirit in the lives of all who serve the Lord in His Church. And we pray that, along with fidelity to a life of prayer, they will properly seek out support, friendship, and study with their brothers and sisters and spiritual direction from those through whom the Spirit may lead them to holiness.

The Assumption

Mary is taken, body and soul, to Heaven. She is gloriously triumphant. But this most loving mother, so beautiful in her triumph, lived a life of deep humility and service to others. And just as Mary cradled and nurtured the infant Jesus in her womb, prayed and pondered, and served Him throughout His life, so does this heavenly mother cradle and nurture every vocation in her Immaculate Heart, always praying and interceding for them.

We pray for all the newly ordained and professed that they will grow in humility, remain faithful to their duties and that, as they turn their face to this loving mother each day, they will find her present in their every need.

The Coronation

Mary is crowned Queen of Heaven and Earth by her Divine Son. She is the "woman clothed with the sun, with the moon under her feet, and on her head a crown of twelve stars."[19] She is "blessed"[20] forever!

We pray for all our brothers and sisters who live their lives in the service of Holy Mother Church, especially the newly ordained and professed, that they will turn to Mary and, imitating her virtues in every circumstance of their lives, come to know with her the reward of their fidelity to Christ.

19. Revelation 12:1   20. Luke 1:48

GENERAL INTERCESSIONS FOR VOCATIONS

(All of the following intercessions may be used or the leader may select from the list)

Leader: For an increase in vocations to the priesthood and consecrated life, that the Master of the Harvest will supply laborers for the harvest, in our own diocese and all around the world, we pray to the Lord. …

All: **Lord hear our prayer.**

Leader: For all young men and women who feel they may be called to the priesthood or consecrated life, that they will pray and discern carefully, trust the Lord, and follow Him with all their hearts, we pray to the Lord …

All: **Lord hear our prayer.**

Leader: For all parents, that they will pray earnestly for vocations in their own family and, through their prayer and example, nourish the call of God in their children. We pray, too, that they will give their blessing and support to a son or daughter who has discerned a vocation. For these, we pray to the Lord …

All: **Lord hear our prayer.**

Leader: For all young men and women now in formation, we pray for courage, trust, and perseverance in prayer as they face any doubts, uncertainties, or obstacles that may come their way, we pray to the Lord …

All: **Lord hear our prayer.**

Leader: For all people of holy faith, that they will be true witnesses to the Gospel, inspiring and inviting young men and women to consider their vocation, and always surrounding the vocations in their midst with love and prayer, we pray to the Lord …

All: **Lord hear our prayer.**

(*Optional*) **Pause to add own intentions for vocations.**

All: Our Father who art in Heaven hallowed be
Thy name; Thy Kingdom come, Thy will be done,
on earth as it is in Heaven. Give us this day our daily
bread and forgive us our trespasses as we forgive
those who trespass against us. And lead us not into
temptation, but deliver us from evil.   Amen.

CONCLUDING PRAYER

Leader: Let us Pray.

All: Lord Jesus, Son of the Eternal Father and Mary
Immaculate, give to our young people the generosity
necessary to follow Your call and the courage required
to overcome all obstacles to their vocation.
Give to parents that faith, love and spirit of sacrifice
which will inspire them to offer their children
to God's service and to rejoice whenever one of their
children is called to the priesthood or religious life.
May Your example and that of Your Blessed Mother
and Saint Joseph encourage both young people
and parents and let Your grace sustain them.

                                        Amen.

Continue to Benediction Hymns and Prayers on page 73

BENEDICTION HYMNS AND PRAYERS

If the prayers of the Holy Hour for Priests or Vocations have been said with Exposition of the Blessed Sacrament, the following Benediction hymn may be sung and prayers said.

"Tantum Ergo"

Tantum ergo Sacramentum,
Veneremur cernui:
Et antiquum documentum
Novo cedat ritui:
Praestet fides supplementum
Sensuum defectui.

Genitori, Genitoque
Laus et jubilatio,
Salus, honor, virtus quoque,
Sit et benedictio:
Procedenti ab utroque
Compar sit laudatio.

Amen.

"Down in Adoration Falling"

Down in adoration falling,
This great Sacrament we hail;
Over ancient forms of worship
Newer rites of grace prevail;
Faith tells us that Christ is present
When our human senses fail.

To the Everlasting Father,
And the Son Who made us free,
And the Spirit, God proceeding
From Them each eternally.
Be salvation, honor, blessing,
Might and endless majesty.

Amen.

Leader: You have given them bread from Heaven.

All: **Having all sweetness within it.**

Leader: Let us pray: Lord Jesus Christ, You gave us the Eucharist as the memorial of Your suffering and death. May our worship of this Sacrament of Your Body and Blood help us to experience the salvation You won for us and the peace of the Kingdom where You live with the Father and the Holy Spirit, God, for ever and ever.

BENEDICTION

A blessing with the monstrance may be given if there is a priest or deacon present.

The Divine Praises

Blessed be God.

Blessed be His Holy Name.

Blessed be Jesus Christ, true God and true Man.

Blessed be the Name of Jesus.

Blessed be His Most Sacred Heart.

Blessed be His Most Precious Blood.

Blessed be Jesus in the Most Holy Sacrament
of the Altar.

Blessed be the Holy Spirit, the Paraclete.

Blessed be the Great Mother of God,
Mary Most Holy.

Blessed be her Holy
and Immaculate Conception.

Blessed be her Glorious Assumption.

Blessed be the Name of Mary,
Virgin and Mother.

Blessed be St. Joseph,
her most chaste spouse.

Blessed be God in His Angels
and in His Saints.

*

May the Heart of Jesus
in the Most Blessed Sacrament
be praised, adored, and loved,
with grateful affection, at every moment,
in all the tabernacles of the world,
even to the end of time.

Amen.

Holy God, We Praise Thy Name

Holy God, we praise Thy Name;
Lord of all, we bow before Thee.
All on earth Thy scepter claim;
All in Heaven above adore Thee.
Infinite Thy vast domain,
Everlasting is Thy reign.
(repeat)

Hark! The loud celestial hymn,
Angel choirs above are raising.
Cherubim and Seraphim
In unceasing chorus praising,
Fill the Heavens with sweet accord
Holy, holy, holy Lord.
(repeat)

THE STATIONS OF THE CROSS
WITH MEDITATIONS ON THE PRIESTHOOD

Introduction

It is not possible for any lay person, male or female, to grasp or comprehend fully the sublime vocation to the Sacred Priesthood of Jesus Christ or what it means to live out this calling.

Each of us, in a very real sense, is called to live our lives walking with Jesus up the hill of Calvary. But it is a deep reality — a deep and sacred reality — that those ordained to the priesthood will, *in persona Christi*, lay down their lives for others.

We, as laity, can never enter fully into the mystery of the life of a priest, but we might, on occasion, discover a "window" through which we catch a glimpse or gain a little deeper understanding of his life as he lives it on the road to Calvary with Jesus.

In writing these short meditations on the priesthood for the Stations of the Cross, we hope to offer you a "window" such as this to look through. As you make the Stations with these meditations, please consider offering them for the sanctification of all priests and their fidelity to their vocation.

The Way of the Cross

The Sign of the Cross (+)

Leader: In the Name of the Father, and of the Son,
and of the Holy Spirit.

All: Amen.

Opening Prayer

All: Lord Jesus Christ, You entrusted Your Church to the
apostles, Your first priests, and willed that they and
those who would follow after them should take up
their Cross and follow You. To this day, this sacrificial
nature of Your Holy Priesthood remains unchanged.

Grant, O Lord, that, through the merits of these
prayers and meditations on Your passion and death,
Your priests may come to love You more deeply and
follow You more faithfully.

We ask this through the Sorrowful and Immaculate
Heart of Mary, the first to make this Way of the Cross
with You.

Amen.

FIRST STATION — Jesus is Condemned to Death

Leader: We adore You, O Christ, and we praise You;

All: **Because by Your Holy Cross,
You have redeemed the world.**

Jesus, in God's plan of salvation, offers His life
on the Cross for us.

Here is the priest at his ordination. It is a wondrous and
happy day — yet, the priest, now *alter Christus*, that is,
another Christ, will offer his life for the sanctification
and salvation of souls.

Leader: Lord Jesus Crucified,
All: **Have mercy on all priests.**

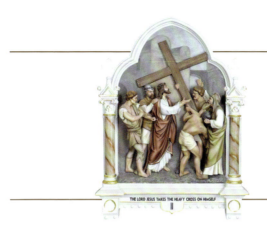

SECOND STATION – Jesus Accepts His Cross

Leader: We adore You, O Christ, and we praise You;

All:　**Because by Your Holy Cross,**
　　　You have redeemed the world.

What a burden is laid on the shoulders of a man as he is ordained – the weight of our sanctification, the obligation to pray and suffer and sacrifice for our good – to do his part to help fill up what is lacking in the sufferings of Christ for the sake of His Church.[1]

Leader: Lord Jesus Crucified,
All:　**Have mercy on all priests.**

1 *Colossians 1:24 (NAB)*

THE LORD JESUS FALLS FOR THE FIRST TIME UNDER THE CROSS

III

THIRD STATION — Jesus Falls the First Time

Leader: We adore You, O Christ, and we praise You;

All: **Because by Your Holy Cross,**
You have redeemed the world.

What is it that caused Jesus to fall the first time? What causes a priest to fall? Could it be that there are so many demands on his time that he begins, little by little, to be torn away from his prayer life, his time with Jesus Who is the source of his strength? Prayer is his oxygen, the very life-breath of his priesthood.

Leader: Lord Jesus Crucified,
All: **Have mercy on all priests.**

THE LORD JESUS MEETS HIS MOTHER

IV

FOURTH STATION — Jesus Meets His Mother
on the Road to Calvary

Leader: We adore You, O Christ, and we praise You;

All: **Because by Your Holy Cross,
You have redeemed the world.**

The sight of Mary consoled Jesus and yet increased His suffering because He knew how painful it was for her to see Him this way.

How necessary it is that every priest look to Mary —
if only to turn his gaze upon her from time to time each day
— and let her motherly smile console and encourage him.

Leader: Lord Jesus Crucified,
All: **Have mercy on all priests.**

FIFTH STATION — Simon of Cyrene is Compelled to Help Jesus Carry His Cross

Leader: We adore You, O Christ, and we praise You;

All: **Because by Your Holy Cross,**
You have redeemed the world.

The word here is "compelled." St. Luke says Simon was "seized" and the Cross was "laid on him." [2]

The priest, one with Jesus, has come to the priesthood willing to embrace the Cross. How often, we, like Simon, have to be "compelled" to carry the Cross with Jesus, even "seized," and then we do so grudgingly.

Leader: Lord Jesus Crucified,
All: **Have mercy on all priests.**

2 Luke 23:26 (RSV)

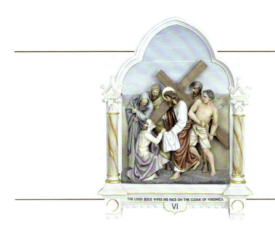

THE LORD JESUS WIPES HIS FACE ON THE CLOAK OF VERONICA

VI

SIXTH STATION — Veronica Wipes the Face of Jesus

Leader: We adore You, O Christ, and we praise You;

All: **Because by Your Holy Cross,**
You have redeemed the world.

Veronica's name literally means "true icon" or "true image."

Every ordained priest, no matter who he is, where he is called
to serve, or how he responds to that call, bears the true image
of Christ — in his face, on his hands, on his very soul.

What can I do to imitate Veronica's kindness to the suffering
Christ? What can I offer a suffering *alter Christus*?

Surely I can offer my prayers, perhaps a fast, perhaps an
encouraging word or some other small kindness or sacrifice.

Leader: Lord Jesus Crucified,
All: **Have mercy on all priests.**

THE LORD JESUS FALLS FOR THE SECOND TIME UNDER THE CROSS

VII

SEVENTH STATION — Jesus Falls a Second Time

Leader: We adore You, O Christ, and we praise You;

All: **Because by Your Holy Cross,**
You have redeemed the world.

A second time, Jesus falls under the weight of the Cross. He is exhausted and in unfathomable pain.

The priest who has been on his priestly journey for some time must be constantly aware of the snares in his path lest he fall into them. Of all these many pitfalls, perhaps the worst is loneliness — for this one can lead him into a host of other dangers.

How very important it is that we pray for priests, especially those who are lonely, and how vital it is that every priest has the company and support of his brother priests. Above all, the priest must immerse himself in Jesus Who alone satisfies, fills the void of loneliness, heals wounds, gives strength, and fills him with love.

Leader: Lord Jesus Crucified,
All: **Have mercy on all priests.**

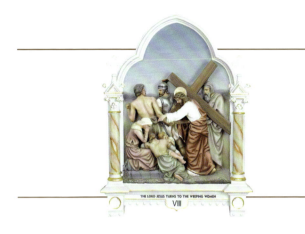

THE LORD JESUS TURNS TO THE WEEPING WOMEN
VIII

EIGHTH STATION — Jesus Meets the Women of Jerusalem

Leader: We adore You, O Christ, and we praise You;

All: **Because by Your Holy Cross,**
You have redeemed the world.

Jesus, in spite of His pain and fatigue, stops to console others along His path.

How often the priest, weary, overwhelmed with responsibilities, struggling perhaps with his own pain, must reach out to ease the pain of others, to console and encourage, to be the mercy and compassion of Jesus at a deathbed, to redirect the course of a repentant sinner. And he may, in the midst of all this, feel acutely his own inadequacy. The road to Calvary is long and uphill.

Leader: Lord Jesus Crucified,
All: **Have mercy on all priests.**

THE LORD JESUS FALLS FOR THE THIRD TIME UNDER THE CROSS

IX

NINTH STATION — Jesus Falls the Third Time

Leader: We adore You, O Christ, and we praise You;

All: **Because by Your Holy Cross,**
You have redeemed the world.

Jesus, near the end of His journey to Calvary, falls yet again. Surrounded by the brutality of the soldiers, He struggles to get up and keep going.

What caused Jesus to fall this third time? What might cause a priest to struggle and fall again and again? And how should we respond?

The priest is truly Jesus on the way to Calvary. When he falls under his burden, the gossip, unkindness and scorn he receives, in truth, fall on Jesus Who is suffering in His struggling brother priest.

Jesus could hear the mockery and scorn of those around Him and so can the priest. Will we love and pray a struggling priest back into service or let our words and actions keep him from getting up again?

Leader: Lord Jesus Crucified,
All: **Have mercy on all priests.**

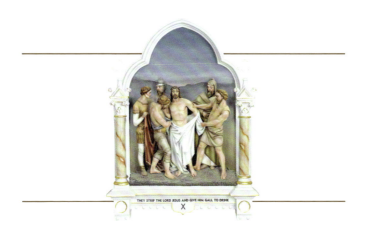

THEY STRIP THE LORD JESUS AND GIVE HIM GALL TO DRINK

X

TENTH STATION — Jesus is Stripped of His Garments

Leader: We adore You, O Christ, and we praise You;

All: **Because by Your Holy Cross,**
You have redeemed the world.

Jesus' seamless tunic is stripped away from Him, causing His wounds to open and bleed. Naked and poor, His glory hidden, He stands before the crowd who does not recognize who He really is.

The priest, too, stands before the people — in sacred vestments, in black suit and collar, in places of honor. He is set apart from others. Still, when all this "covering" is taken away — when he is imprisoned by godless regimes and stripped of his freedom, when he has grown old and is stripped of his health and ability to serve, perhaps even when he has fallen into sin and is stripped of his own dignity — yet, he remains clothed in the sacred "garment" of the priesthood, and so shall he be for all eternity.

Leader: Lord Jesus Crucified,
All: **Have mercy on all priests.**

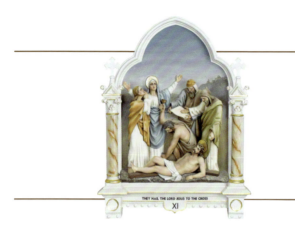

THEY NAIL THE LORD JESUS TO THE CROSS

XI

ELEVENTH STATION — Jesus is Nailed to the Cross

Leader: We adore You, O Christ, and we praise You;

All: **Because by Your Holy Cross,
You have redeemed the world.**

Jesus is nailed to the Cross. He hangs in agony, suspended between Heaven and Earth, suspended between two thieves — the one who reviles Him with disdain and the other who begs for mercy.

The priest, also nailed to the Cross by the very sacrificial nature of the priesthood, is suspended between Heaven, which he experiences in the Mass, and earth, which he experiences in the daily living out of his vocation. He, too, experiences those who revile and ridicule him and those who beg for mercy. United to Jesus, he must turn his gaze to the Father in Heaven.

Leader: Lord Jesus Crucified,
All: **Have mercy on all priests..**

TWELFTH STATION — Jesus Dies on the Cross

Leader: We adore You, O Christ, and we praise You;

All: **Because by Your Holy Cross,
You have redeemed the world.**

Jesus, having accomplished all that the Father sent Him to do, says, "It is finished." [3]
"Father, into Your Hands I commend My Spirit." [4]

Every priest comes to his ordination day with a sense of purpose and a desire to do the Will of the Father. And every priest hopes to approach his death with a sense of having accomplished all that he was given to do so that he may unite himself with Jesus saying, "It is finished ... Father, into Your Hands I commend my spirit."

Leader: Lord Jesus Crucified,
All: **Have mercy on all priests.**

3 *John 19:30 (NAB)*   4 *Luke 23:46 (NAB)*

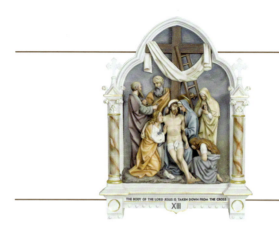

THIRTEENTH STATION — The Body of Jesus is Taken Down from the Cross and Placed in the Arms of His Mother

Leader: We adore You, O Christ, and we praise You;

All: **Because by Your Holy Cross,
You have redeemed the world.**

Jesus' "hour" had finally come.[5] It will come for every priest, too. And as Mary receives each priest as a special son on the day of his ordination and remains at his side throughout his life of ministry, so shall she receive into her arms every faithful son at the hour of his death.

Leader: Lord Jesus Crucified,
All: **Have mercy on all priests.**

5 *John 17:1 (NAB)*

THE BODY OF THE LORD JESUS IS BROUGHT TO THE TOMB

XIV

FOURTEENTH STATION — Jesus is Laid in the Tomb

Leader: We adore You, O Christ, and we praise You;

All: **Because by Your Holy Cross,**
You have redeemed the world.

Jesus has completed His ministry on earth. By His Cross and Resurrection, He has set us free. He is the Savior of the World.

The priest, like Jesus, will go to the tomb someday. Through the power of the Cross and Resurrection of Jesus, he, too, through his ministry, has been able to set people free — free from their sins, free to recognize Jesus as Savior, free to enter into the Kingdom of God.

Leader: Lord Jesus Crucified,
All: **Have mercy on all priests.**

PRAYERS FOR THE HOLY FATHER

All: Our Father,
           Hail Mary,
           Glory Be

CONCLUDING PRAYER

All: Almighty and Eternal Father, we, Your children, lift up
           to You our prayers for our priests. We beg You to bless
           them and fill them with strength and perseverance as
           they take up their cross each day. Grant them to
           be faithful disciples of Christ the High Priest. Lead
           them as they lead us that we may all attain to eternal
           salvation. Grant this through Christ our Lord.

                                                        Amen.

THE RESURRECTION

APPENDIX

Scripture Passages Grouped by Liturgical Season

READINGS FOR THE ADVENT SEASON

Option 1 - *Isaiah 25:6-9*
Option 2 - *Romans 1:1-7*

READINGS FOR THE CHRISTMAS SEASON

Option 1 - *Colossians 1:15-29*
Option 2 - *Isaiah 62:6-12*

READINGS FOR THE LENTEN SEASON

Option 1 - *2 Corinthians 5:17-6:10*
Option 2 - *Luke 22:14-20*

READINGS FOR THE EASTER SEASON

Option 1 - *Luke 24:13-35*
Option 2 - *John 20:19-23*
Option 3 - *John 21:15-19*

READINGS FOR ORDINARY TIME

Option 1 - *Genesis 14:18-20*
Option 2 - *Hebrews 4:14-5:10*
Option 3 - *Mark 10:42-45*
Option 4 - *1 Timothy 6:6-16*
Option 5 - *2 Timothy 4:1-8*
Option 6 - *1 Peter 5:1-4, 8-11*

WORKS CITED

Catholic Church, Directory on the Life and Ministry of Priests.
Vatican City: *Libreria Editrice Vaticana*, 1994.

Catholic Church, *Rosarium Virginis Mariae*.
Vatican City: *Libreria Editrice Vaticana*, 2002.

Diary of St. Maria Faustina Kowalska:
Divine Mercy in My Soul, Copyright 1987
Congregation of Marians of the Immaculate Conception
Stockbridge, MA 01263.
Used with permission.

Ignatius Bible, Revised Standard Version. San Francisco, CA:
Ignatius Press, Catholic Edition of the New Testament,
Copyright 1965; Catholic Edition of the Old Testament,
incorporating the Apocrypha, 1966.

New American Bible, St. Joseph's Edition. New York, NY:
Catholic Book Publishing, 1992.

Opus Bono Prayer for the Urgent Needs of Priests
Opus Bono Sacerdotii (opusbono.org)
Used with Permission

Pope Francis
World Meeting of Families
September 2015, Philadelphia, PA, USA

Serra Prayer for Vocations. USA Council of Serra International.
Used with permission.

REFERENCES FOR THE ROSARY FOR PRIESTS

1   Pope Francis, World Meeting of Families

2   See Ephesians 3:15

3   Opus Bono Prayer for the Urgent Needs of Priests

4   Hebrews 7:17 (NAB*)

5   Luke 2:25 (NAB)

6   Luke 2:34 (NAB)

7   Luke 2:52 (NAB)

8   Rosarium Virginis Mariae, 21

9   John 1:29 (NAB)

10   John 2:3 (NAB)

11   John 2:5 (NAB)

12   Mark 1:15 (NAB)

13   Luke 22:42 (RSV†)

14   Isaiah 53:3,7 (RSV)

15   Matthew 28:19 (NAB)

16   Directory on the Ministry and Life of Priests, 9

17   John 19:26 (NAB)

18   Divine Mercy in My Soul, (Diary, #1052)
Diary of St. Maria Faustina Kowalska:
Divine Mercy in My Soul © 1987 Congregation of Marians
of the Immaculate Conception, Stockbridge, MA 01263
Used with permission.

BIBLICAL REFERENCES FOR THE ROSARY
FOR VOCATIONS

1 John 12:24
2 Luke 1:34
3 Luke 1:38
4 Luke 1:43, 45
5 Luke 2:25
6 Luke 2:37
7 Luke 2:46
8 Mark 1:10-11
9 John 2:3
10 John 2:5
11 Matthew 4:19
12 Matthew 17:4
13 Matthew 26:26-28
14 Psalms 57:7
15 Matthew 26:39
16 Luke 22:19
17 John 12:24
18 Matthew 28:19-20
19 Revelation 12:1
20 Luke 1:48

BIBLICAL REFERENCES FOR
THE STATIONS OF THE CROSS

1 Colossians 1:24 (NAB)
2 Luke 23:26 (RSV)
3 John 19:30 (NAB)
4 Luke 23:46 (NAB)
5 John 17:1 (NAB)

Notes

PRAYING FOR OUR PRIESTS
ORDER FORM

☐ **YES! I would like to order the following prayer resources to Pray for Our Priests!**

No.　　**Prayer Resource**

_____　Praying for Our Priests books

　　　　Includes Rosary for Priests
　　　　Rosary for Vocations
　　　　Stations of the Cross

_____　Praying for Our Priests Rosary CD (2 CD Set)

_____　Stations of the Cross for Priests (CD)
　　　　Includes Chaplet of Divine Mercy
　　　　And the Litany of the Precious Blood

_____　Praying for Our Priests Prayer Cards — English

_____　Praying for Our Priests Prayer Cards — Spanish

_____　Praying for Our Priests Rosary, Leaflet, Spanish

_____　Stations of the Cross for Priests, Leaflet, Spanish

☐ **YES! I would like to help the apostolate of Maria Regina Cleri print and distribute the book PRAYING FOR OUR PRIESTS and its other prayer resources to as many people as possible. Enclosed is my free will offering of $ _____**

Please fill out the reverse side and mail in the enclosed envelop.
You may also order from our website, www.prayingforourpriests.org.

GOD BLESS YOU!

Name: _____

Address: _____

City _____ State _____ Zip: _____

E-mail Address: _____

Phone: _____

Maria
Regina
Cleri™

P.O. BOX 540657, OMAHA, NE 68154

103

P.O. BOX 540657, OMAHA, NE 68154

To order bulk quantities of books or CDs produced by Maria Regina Cleri for yourself, parish, prayer group, or other organization, simply visit our website at:

www.prayingforourpriests.org

GOD BLESS YOU!

MARIA REGINA CLERI

P.O. BOX 540657

OMAHA, NE 68154